**W9-BNT-503**

Routes of Science

Atoms and Molecules

Chris Woodford and Martin Clowes

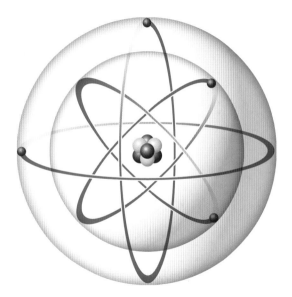

BLACKBIRCH®
PRESS

THOMSON
✳
™
GALE

San Diego • Detroit • New York • San Francisco • Cleveland • New Haven, Conn. • Waterville, Maine • London • Munich

THOMSON

GALE

Every effort has been made to trace
the owners of copyrighted material.

PHOTOGRAPHIC CREDITS
Cover: University of Pennsylvania
Library/Smith Image Collection (l);
National Library of Medicine (t);
Science Photo Library/Clive Freeman,
Biosym Technologies (b).

CERN: 34; **Corbis:** Bettmann 22, 35t, John
Wilkes Studio 10, 11b, Layne Kennedy 8,
Wally McNamee 36; **DaimlerChrysler:** 23;
Dynamic Graphics: 14l; **Getty Images:** Hulton
Archive 11t; **Hemera Photo Objects:** 27r;
Mary Evans Picture Library: 7, 7b, 15; **NASA:**
37; **National Library of Medicine:** 28r;
Photodisc: 6; **Science Photo Library:** Clive
Freeman/Biosym Technologies 14tr, Dr. Gary
Gaugler 12, Alfred Pasieka 27l, J. C. Revy 29t;
Topham Picturepoint: 28l; **University of
Pennsylvania Library:** Smith Collection 13b,
16, 17t, 17b, 18t, 20, 23b, 25, 29b, 30, 35t.

Consultant: Don Franceschetti, Ph.D.,
   Distinguished Service Professor,
   Departments of Physics and Chemistry,
   The University of Memphis,
   Memphis, Tennessee

For The Brown Reference Group plc
Text: Chris Woodford and Martin Clowes
Editor: John Jackson
Designer: Iain Stuart
Picture Researcher: Helen Simm
Illustrators: Darren Awuah,
   Richard Burgess, and Mark Walker
Managing Editor: Bridget Giles
Art Director: Dave Goodman
Children's Publisher: Anne O'Daly
Production Director: Alastair Gourlay
Editorial Director: Lindsey Lowe

LIBRARY OF CONGRESS CATALOGING-IN-PUBLICATION DATA

Woodford, Chris.
   Atoms and Molecules / by Chris Woodford and Martin Clowes.
      p. cm. -- (Routes of science)
Includes bibliographical references and index.
Contents: Philosophers and alchemists – Discovering the elements – The periodic
table – Molecules, matter, and motion – Inside the atom – Into the future.
   ISBN 1-4103-0295-4 (hardback : alk. paper)
   1. Atoms and molecules--Juvenile literature. [1. Atoms – 2. Molecules.] I. Title. II.
Series.

Printed and bound in Singapore
10 9 8 7 6 5 4 3 2 1

CONTENTS

INTRODUCTION

Matter is the scientific name for the material that makes up everything around us—ourselves, the air we breathe, the ground on which we stand, and everything we can touch or smell. Matter is formed by atoms and molecules.

MATTER IS ALL AROUND US. IT is formed by individual atoms that are many thousands of times too small to see through a microscope. Atoms are such tiny structures that until the twentieth century, scientists had no firm proof that they even existed.

The notion that matter might consist of atoms occurred to a few Greek philosophers almost two thousand five hundred years ago. The idea did not catch on. Most Greek philosophers believed four or five basic substances combined to produce all matter. Their theory had no place for atoms.

The theory of atoms resurfaced in the late seventeenth century when chemists started to work in an organized way. They found several basic substances that they could not split into simpler substances. Chemists called these substances chemical elements.

Centuries passed before scientists formulated modern ideas about the atoms that formed the elements.

The idea that atoms join to make larger, more complicated structures called molecules first appeared in the nineteenth century. The theory of molecules not only helps us understand why many chemical substances behave as they do but also explains why solids, liquids, and gases behave differently from one another.

Modern theories about the structure of atoms emerged around the start of the twentieth century. Physicists then discovered the fragments that make up atoms: electrons, neutrons, and protons.

Experiments suggested that neutrons and protons clump together at the core of each atom in a tight bundle, called the nucleus. Scientists then set about determining how electrons fit in or around the nucleus.

Quantum theory explores the structure of individual atoms and explains how atoms group together to form molecules. The science of quantum mechanics has enabled chemists to predict and then discover new substances with unusual and useful properties. Physicists have been exploring electrons, neutrons, and protons to see if they consist of yet smaller bits of matter.

1 PHILOSOPHERS AND ALCHEMISTS

The ancient Greek philosophers believed that matter consisted of mixtures of four or five basic elements (substances). Later, alchemists tried to turn common metals, such as lead, into precious gold.

ANCIENT GREEK PHILOSOPHERS developed theories of matter based on what they saw around them. In the ninth century B.C., (Thales of Miletus) noticed that all living things need water to survive. He suggested water was the basis of all matter. Anaximander (610–c.547 B.C.), a student of Thales,

Thales of Miletus

Greek philosophers did not conduct experiments but studied the world around them. The founder of Greek philosophy, Thales (c. 625–c. 550 B.C.), had many interests. Not only did he realize that water was essential to life, he also investigated cosmology and surveying. He studied the path of the Moon and gained great respect when, in 585 B.C., he predicted a solar eclipse accurately. Thales died when he fell off a cliff as he gazed at the stars.

The Elements

Most Greek philosophers' theories of matter featured the idea of four basic substances called elements: fire, air, water, and earth. Anaximenes (570–500 B.C.) believed air was the key element. He thought pressure turned air into water (below), then earth, and finally stone. Around 450 B.C., Empedocles (490–430 B.C.) suggested all substances were blends of the four elements. Aristotle, who lived a century later, proposed a fifth element called ether.

The Beginning of Atoms

The first person to propose the existence of atoms was the Greek philosopher Leucippus (c. 450–370 B.C.). His student, Democritus (right), developed the idea around 450 B.C., when he suggested that matter was made of tiny indestructible particles that he called atoma, Greek for "uncuttables." Democritus believed that different kinds of atoms made different kinds of matter. He thought that smooth atoms formed liquids and jagged ones locked together as solids.

modified Thales's theory by suggesting the existence of a universal substance called apeiron. Apeiron was thought to contain all possible opposites, such as hot and cold, and wet and dry. According to the theory, a pebble might be a mixture of the cold, hard, and dry parts of apeiron. Other substances might be combinations of the hot, soft, and wet parts of apeiron.

In the fifth century B.C. two philosophers proposed that matter consisted of (atoms.) Their theory was later sidelined when the famous philosopher Aristotle (384–322 B.C.) returned to the theory of (elements.) Aristotle believed fire, air, water, and earth made up all matter on Earth, and that the sky and beyond were made of a fifth element called ether.

Precious and Base Metals

Gold (right) and silver occur naturally. They were very rare commodities until people learned to release pure metals from their ores (the raw state in which they occur in nature). Their rarity and shining beauty, combined with the ease with which they can be fashioned into coins, ornaments, and utensils, made gold and silver valued as precious metals. Lead is useful but was never considered precious. It is easy to extract lead from plentiful ores. The dark, dull metal is easily shaped, which makes it useful for practical applications such as plumbing and roofing. Lead tarnishes quickly and has less glamorous uses than silver or gold, so it is an example of a base metal.

No one knows exactly how alchemy began, but it is certain that people have worked with metals for many thousands of years. The ancient Chinese believed gold could make someone live longer. This belief drove their attempts to produce gold from (base metals) such as lead. Later alchemists tried to turn lead into gold to make money for themselves or their sponsors. Turning one substance into another was known as transmutation. Transmutation also applied to changing sickness to health and old age to youth. Alchemists sought ways to realize all these goals.

Alchemists often worked in secret and enacted rituals that combined ancient myths with religion and (astrology.) Alchemists used symbols, rhymes, and codes to protect their methods from competitors. Some alchemists reported success in making gold from less valuable substances, but the records of their methods are often impossible to understand. Chemists now know that no chemical reaction can make gold from another element. The alchemists who claimed they could make gold were bluffing or fooling themselves. By the late fourth century B.C., alchemy had reached Alexandria, an Egyptian city near the mouth of the Nile River. Alexandrian alchemists adopted Aristotle's theory of the four earthly elements. The result was a new form of alchemy based on fire, air, water, and earth. Alexandrian alchemy later spread to Europe. Some renowned scientists, including Isaac Newton, were secret alchemists.

Metals and Planets

The alchemists of the fourth century B.C. linked each of the planets and the Sun and Moon with metals. Often the associations reflected the appearance of both items: The Sun was linked with gold, the Moon with silver, and the rust-colored planet Mars with iron. Other planets and many more metals have since been discovered.

Planet	Sun	Mercury	Venus	Moon	Mars	Jupiter	Saturn	Uranus	Neptune	Pluto
Metal	Gold	Mercury	Copper	Silver	Iron	Tin	Lead	None	None	None

Above: Alchemists associated the planets with metals, but their knowledge of heavenly bodies and chemical elements was far from complete. The outer planets—Uranus, Neptune, and Pluto—were unknown to the alchemists of two thousand four hundred years ago.

2 DISCOVERING THE ELEMENTS

In the late seventeenth century, chemists started to move away from alchemy. Their experiments became more thorough and accurate, and chemists soon began to understand more about the workings of matter.

THE ALCHEMISTS FAILED IN their quests to turn lead into gold and produce an elixir of life that would make people live forever.

Despite their questionable aims and methods, alchemists paved the way for modern chemistry by creating recipes for making useful chemicals such as

Phosphorus

Hennig Brand thought he might get gold from urine because of their similar colors. He boiled urine down to a paste, mixed it with sand, and heated the mixture. The vapors cooled to give a waxy solid that glowed in air and sometimes caught fire. Brand called this material phosphorus, which is Greek for "bringer of light." Phosphorus is now extracted from rocks.

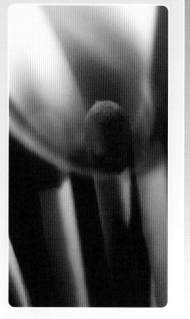

Phosphorus is a main ingredient in match heads.

Element

To an alchemist, the elements were fire, air, water, and earth. Modern chemists use the same word to describe the components of all substances. A chemical element cannot be separated into a simpler form by chemical processes. An element can be divided physically into atoms without altering its basic chemical properties (*see* page 21).

The Skeptical Chemist

In 1661 Irish-born Robert Boyle (1627–1691; right) wrote a book called *The Skeptical Chemist*. The word *chemist* was a shortened version of "alchemist" and caught on as the term for people who study chemicals. In his article, Boyle correctly proposed elements as the simplest forms of matter that could be detected by chemical tests. Boyle thought that gases consisted of small particles surrounded by space. This idea fitted with the ancient Greek Democritus's atomic model of matter. When Boyle found that rusting metals gained weight, he realized correctly that particles in the metal were combining with particles in air.

alcohol, ammonia, and acids. Later chemists used these materials in their experiments. Alchemists also developed techniques for separating mixtures into individual substances. Some alchemists' achievements were strokes of luck. In 1669 the German alchemist (Hennig Brand) discovered phosphorus by chance as he searched for gold in urine. People were amazed by phosphorus because it glowed in the dark and ignited. It was the first new (element) to be discovered for more than a century. The discovery came a few years after (Robert Boyle) suggested there must be more elements than just fire, air, water, and earth. Alchemists thought smoke was a form of air. Boyle knew differently: He found it was composed of soot, moisture, and tars.

The Champion of Phlogiston

German scientist Georg Stahl (1660–1734) went to great lengths to defend his theory of phlogiston against critics. One of Stahl's suggestions was that the form of phlogiston lost during corrosion must have negative weight. He came up with this strange theory to explain why substances such as iron gain weight when they corrode.

Rust

The theory of phlogiston interrupted scientific progress. Robert Boyle had already proposed that rusting was the combination of iron with particles in the air. He was correct. Iron combines with oxygen from the air to produce the rough and reddish substance called rust, shown here magnified many times.

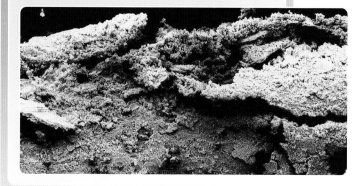

Robert Boyle's idea that particles of different substances combined during rusting was correct. Rusting is an example of a chemical reaction. Boyle reported his experiments in accurate detail, unlike the alchemists before him who guarded their secrets. Some historians hail Boyle as the first true chemist. After Boyle died, the development of chemistry into its modern form was hampered by a false theory. In 1703 Georg Stahl proposed the existence of phlogiston. He got the name from the Greek word *phlogistos*, meaning "inflammable." He believed burning and rusting were the same process at different speeds. Stahl thought that ashes or rust remained when all phlogiston had escaped from a material. Phlogiston theory persisted for more than a century. A number of scientists supported the theory through their own findings. In 1766 the British scientist Henry Cavendish (1731–1810) suggested that phlogiston was the inflammable air that forms when acids corrode metals. The idea seemed to make sense to Cavendish because it linked burning to corrosion. We now know inflammable air as hydrogen.

British chemist Joseph Priestley (1733–1804) isolated a gas from air in 1774. He noted that substances burned more brightly in the new gas than they did in air. Priestley concluded that the new gas was lacking in phlogiston and named it "dephlogisticated air."

Antoine-Laurent Lavoisier, a French chemist, destroyed phlogiston theory in 1777. He burned samples of sulfur

Antoine-Laurent Lavoisier

Lavoisier (right; holding flask) was born in Paris in 1743. As a youth he boasted that he was destined for glory. It was no exaggeration: The many discoveries he made have prompted some people to call him the father of modern chemistry. Lavoisier also became a very rich man. In later life Lavoisier used his chemical knowledge to improve farming methods and the manufacture of gunpowder. He also worked on tax reform. Rich people became very unpopular during the French Revolution. In 1794 revolutionaries executed Lavoisier by guillotine.

The Caloric Theory

Scientists once believed that heat was caused by a mysterious invisible fluid called caloric. They thought that a piece of metal heats up when it is beaten with a hammer because hot caloric flows out of it. What really causes the heat is energy transferred from the hammer blows. Similarly, heat from exercise is not the release of caloric but heat energy released from working muscles (right).

Compounds

A compound is a substance made from two or more elements. Water (shown in the model below) is a compound of hydrogen and oxygen; ammonia is a compound of hydrogen and nitrogen. Compounds form when elements or other compounds join during a chemical reaction. The links that hold elements and compounds together are called chemical bonds.

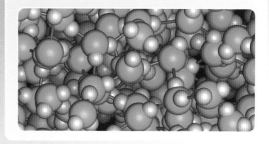

and phosphorus and weighed the products. Lavoisier discovered that the products were heavier than the initial samples. The increase in weight came from the air. Lavoisier realized that the burning elements were not releasing phlogiston, but combining with the gas then called dephlogisticated air. Lavoisier renamed the gas oxygène (oxygen) after the Greek for "acid maker," because the products of

burning phosphorus and sulfur dissolved in water to form acids. Like Boyle, Lavoisier worked in an organized way and reported his work clearly. He discovered many chemical elements and made a list of thirty-three. Two were not elements—light and (caloric,) or heat. Eight were (compounds) that he failed to break down into their basic elements. The rest were true chemical elements.

By the end of the eighteenth century, chemists knew that common substances such as water were made from elements joined as compounds. Scientists proved this fact by breaking compounds apart into the chemical elements that made them up. In 1799 (Humphry Davy) (1778–1829) discovered that by passing an electrical current through some compounds in a process now called (electrolysis,) he could separate them into their component elements.

The Gas Man

British chemist Humphry Davy, shown here giving a lecture, is most famous for developing the Davy lamp. The lamp was a safety light for miners that replaced open flames such as candles. The Davy lamp did not ignite the explosive gases that often build up in coal mines. Davy's simple invention saved the lives of many hundreds of miners. A lifetime of breathing dangerous gases in his chemistry lab is believed to have cost Davy his own life. He became seriously ill in 1827 and died after a heart attack two years later.

Davy Discovers Electrolysis

Davy placed two pieces of metal called electrodes into a jar of water and wired them to a battery cell. As the electric current flowed between the electrodes, the water split into its two elements, hydrogen and oxygen, which were given off as gases. Davy used the same method to separate other substances and discovered new elements, including potassium and sodium. Using electricity to separate compounds became known as electrolysis.

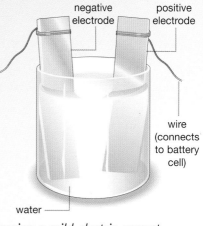

Passing a mild electric current through water can separate the liquid into hydrogen and oxygen.

3 THE PERIODIC TABLE

Chemists such as Humphry Davy split many compounds into their component elements. Along the way, they discovered many new elements. Now chemists needed to find out how the elements related to one another.

SOME SCIENTISTS FOLLOWED Lavoisier and tried to understand elements by studying chemical reactions. In 1794, French chemist Joseph-Louis Proust (1754–1826) formulated his law of constant composition. The law states that the ratios of weights of elements in a

John Dalton: Father of Atomic Theory

After many years of careful scientific research, English scientist John Dalton (1766–1844; right) devised the atomic theory of matter. This was one of the most important scientific theories of all time. Before Dalton, scientists thought that all atoms were the same. Dalton realized that each element had a different atom. He also suggested that all atoms of any one element had the same mass (amount of matter). Dalton's ideas were not entirely correct, but chemists continued to use them for much of the nineteenth century.

Dalton Pictures the Elements

John Dalton used circular symbols (below) to represent the different elements. Some years later, Swedish chemist Jöns Jakob Berzelius (1779–1848) developed the modern system of chemical symbols based on letters and numbers. The letters represented the elements, such as H for hydrogen. The numbers declared the ratios between the elements. Water is H_2O, which explains that two parts of hydrogen (H_2) combine with one part of oxygen (O) to form water.

Dalton Versus Gay-Lussac

The work of Gay-Lussac (right) suggested Dalton's ideas were incomplete or wrong. Dalton saw this as a threat to his new atomic theory and did his best to discredit Gay-Lussac. Dalton claimed Gay-Lussac's measurements were poor and said he could not "admit the French doctrine" and accept Gay-Lussac's ideas.

compound are always the same. For example, hydrogen and oxygen always join in the same proportions to form water. British scientist John Dalton realized that the proportions of elements in a compound would be the same if each element consisted of particles, or atoms, with a fixed size and mass. Dalton published his theory in 1803, together with a list of atomic masses for twelve elements. Dalton believed that simple compounds formed when one particle of each element joined to make one particle of the final product. Frenchman Joseph Louis Gay-Lussac (1778–1850) disagreed. In 1809 he found that when two gases react together, the ratio of

17

Amedeo Avogadro

Amedeo Avogadro (1776–1856; right) was one of the greatest chemists of his time but others, including Dalton and Gay-Lussac, did not accept his theories. Avogadro's work fell into disfavor. Only after he was dead did scientists come to realize the true significance of Avogadro's groundbreaking work.

elements in the resulting compound varies depending on which gases are involved. For example, two volumes of hydrogen gas combine with one volume of oxygen gas to make two volumes of water. This puzzled Dalton. He could not see how three particles of hydrogen and oxygen could form two of water.

In 1811 (Amedeo Avogadro) realized that Dalton had confused the idea of an atom with that of a molecule. Dalton knew that an atom is the smallest possible amount of an element. He did not realize that atoms of some elements join with themselves to form (molecules.) Dalton thought

Splitting the Molecule?

A molecule is the smallest possible amount of a compound. It cannot be split without breaking up the molecule into its constituent chemical elements. If you take a glass of water and throw half away, that leaves half a glass of water. If you divide it in two again and again, you end up with half the amount of water each time, but the substance is still water. Eventually there comes a point when there is one molecule (right) of water left. To reduce the amount of water further would involve breaking the water molecule into its component hydrogen and oxygen atoms. At that point the substance is no longer the compound water, it is hydrogen and oxygen. Elements can also join with themselves and make molecules. For example, a single molecule of oxygen gas is formed by two atoms of oxygen.

WATER MOLECULE

oxygen atom

hydrogen atoms

Avogadro's Law

Avogadro wondered what would happen if he took large empty jars and filled them up with different gases at the same temperature and pressure. He realized that at the same temperature, volume, and pressure, all gases would always contain equal numbers of molecules. The principle applied no matter what gases he put in the jars. It became known as Avogadro's law.

Avogadro's Number

Avogadro knew the number of molecules would be equal at the same volume, temperature, and pressure for any gas, but he could not know how many molecules that was because his equipment was nowhere near sensitive enough. Scientists later found that the number of molecules in two grams of hydrogen is around 600,000,000,000,000,000,000,000. This huge number became known as Avogadro's number. It is such a large number that is almost impossible to picture. If the entire surface of the United States were covered in grains of sand to a depth of about 6 feet (2 m), the number of sand grains would be similar to Avogadro's number. If a machine started to count the sand grains at a rate of one per second, it would take 20,000 trillion years to reach Avogadro's number.

that one atom of hydrogen and one atom of oxygen combined to form one particle of the compound water. Avogadro realized one molecule of two oxygen atoms combined with two molecules of two hydrogen atoms to make two parts of water. He was the first person to realize the crucial difference between an atom and a molecule. Avogadro's other discoveries include (**Avogadro's law.**) The law states that equal volumes of different gases at the same temperature and pressure always contain the same number of molecules. The weight varies between different gases, but the number of molecules is always the same. It became known as (**Avogadro's number.**)

Relative Atomic Mass

Atoms and molecules are extremely small. Measuring the mass of a single molecule or atom involves working with tiny numbers and using sensitive equipment. An easier way is to compare the mass of atoms with a known amount: Scientists currently use a system based on one-twelfth of the mass of a carbon atom. The makes the relative atomic mass of a hydrogen atom, the smallest atom, 1. Helium, the next smallest atom, is 4 times as heavy as hydrogen and is given a relative atomic mass of 4. One atom of uranium is around 238 times as heavy as a hydrogen atom, and its atomic mass is 238.

Mendeleyev

Mendeleyev set out a table of elements in order of their increasing relative atomic mass. He started with hydrogen, the smallest. Next he cut the list into rows and stacked similar elements together in columns. Mendeleyev had produced the first periodic table using rows, or periods, and columns, or groups of elements.

Avogadro's work gave scientists a good idea of the number of atoms or molecules contained in everyday amounts of common substances. According to Avogadro's number, 0.4 ounces (12 g) of the most common form of carbon holds more than six hundred thousand million million million carbon atoms (600, 000, 000, 000, 000, 000, 000, 000).

Avogadro's work was neglected until another Italian, Stanislao Cannizzaro (1826–1910), revived his ideas. Cannizzaro realized that Avogadro's law could be applied to compare the mass of different atoms and molecules. This idea was called (**relative atomic mass**). Relative atomic mass was a simple way of comparing different elements and it revolutionized chemistry.

Chemical knowledge was growing fast. By the 1860s, chemists had discovered sixty-three chemical elements. They wondered what these elements had in common and how they were related to one another. Russian chemist (**Dmitri Mendeleyev**) (1834–1907) solved the puzzle in 1869. He compared the properties of different elements and came up with the (**periodic table**.) There were gaps in the original table, but Mendeleyev was confident enough to not only claim that the gaps would be filled when chemists discovered new elements but also to predict the chemical properties of the unknown elements. Later scientists proved Mendeleyev was right.

The Periodic Table

The periodic table has been updated many time since Mendeleyev's time. Newly discovered elements were added and the positions of some elements were moved around as chemists learned more about the elements and their properties.

Key:
- hydrogen
- alkali metals
- alkaline-earth metals
- transition metals
- lanthanides
- actinides
- noble gases
- nonmetals
- semimetals
- poor metals

1 HYDROGEN																	2 HELIUM
3 LITHIUM	4 BERYLLIUM											5 BORON	6 CARBON	7 NITROGEN	8 OXYGEN	9 FLUORINE	10 NEON
11 SODIUM	12 MAGNES-IUM											13 ALUMINUM	14 SILICON	15 PHOSPHOR-US	16 SULFUR	17 CHLORINE	18 ARGON
19 POTASSIUM	20 CALCIUM	21 SCANDIUM	22 TITANIUM	23 VANADIUM	24 CHROMIUM	25 MANGA-NESE	26 IRON	27 COBALT	28 NICKEL	29 COPPER	30 ZINC	31 GALLIUM	32 GERMANIUM	33 ARSENIC	34 SELENIUM	35 BROMINE	36 KRYPTON
37 RUBIDIUM	38 STRONTIUM	39 YTTRIUM	40 ZIRCON-IUM	41 NIOBIUM	42 MOLYB-DENUM	43 TECHNET-IUM	44 RUTHEN-IUM	45 RHODIUM	46 PALLAD-IUM	47 SILVER	48 CADMIUM	49 INDIUM	50 TIN	51 ANTIMONY	52 TELLURIUM	53 IODINE	54 XENON
55 CAESIUM	56 BARIUM	57–70	71 LUTETIUM	72 HAFNIUM	73 TANTALUM	74 TUNGSTEN	75 RHENIUM	76 OSMIUM	77 IRIDIUM	78 PLATINUM	79 GOLD	80 MERCURY	81 THALLIUM	82 LEAD	83 BISMUTH	84 POLONIUM	85 ASTATINE	84 RADON
87 FRANCIUM	88 RADIUM	89–102	103 LAWRENC-IUM	104 RUTHER-FORDIUM	105 DUBNIUM	106 SEABORG-IUM	107 BOHRIUM	108 HAFFIUM	109 MEITNER-IUM	110 UNUNNIL-IUM	111 UNUNUN-IUM	112 UNUN-BIUM		114 UNUNQUAD-IUM		116 UNUNHEX-IUM		118 UNUNOC-TIUM

Numerals are each element's atomic number. This is the number of protons (*see* page 33) an atom has.

57 LANTHANUM	58 CERIUM	59 PRASEODY-MIUM	60 NEODYM-IUM	61 PROMETH-IUM	62 SAMARIUM	63 EUROPIUM	64 GADOLIN-IUM	65 TERBIUM	66 DYSPROS-IUM	67 HOLMIUM	68 ERBIUM	69 THULIUM	70 YTTERBIUM
89 ACTINIUM	90 THORIUM	91 PROTACTIN-IUM	92 URANIUM	93 NEPTUNIUM	94 PLUTONIUM	95 AMERICIUM	96 CURIUM	97 BERKELIUM	98 CALIFORN-IUM	99 EINSTEIN-IUM	100 FERMIUM	101 MENDELEV-IUM	102 NOBELIUM

4 MOLECULES, MATTER, AND MOTION

Avogadro's law helped chemists think in terms of molecules, but they still did not know how molecules behave and how they are arranged. Understanding the behavior and arrangement of molecules was the crucial next step.

KINETIC THEORY ANSWERED many puzzles for chemists. It was developed in the nineteenth century from Avogadro's ideas by a brilliant group of scientists, notably British physicist James Clerk Maxwell (1831–1879) and Austrian physicist **Ludwig Boltzmann** (1844–1906).

Ludwig Boltzmann

Ludwig Boltzmann (below) moved frequently from one university job to another. Boltzmann suffered from an illness called bipolar disorder. His condition caused his moods to swing back and forth from wild happiness and action to great despair and inactivity. Boltzmann killed himself in 1906, at the age of sixty-two, possibly because he feared his theories on kinetics were about to be proved wrong. After Boltzmann's death, his ideas were accepted as being among the most important contributions to twentieth-century chemistry and physics.

Kinetic Theory

Kinetic theory is the study of the movements of molecules. Molecules in all substances move about. In solids they vibrate in position, and in gases they whiz around freely. How much they move depends on the temperature. The molecules vibrate or move around more when a substance heats up. Kinetic theory also links heat and pressure. The pressure of a gas is due to collisions between the molecules and the container walls. The higher the temperature, the greater the speed of the molecules. Speedier molecules are more likely to hit the walls more often. More collisions mean more pressure.

Thermodynamics

Chemical reactions often cause heat or cooling. Thermodynamics explains how heat energy is taken in or released during a chemical reaction. More than just a theory, thermodynamics has many practical uses. These include working out how to make chemical reactions happen more easily and calculating how to make engines more efficient by converting more fuel into useful power (right).

Kinetic theory made an important connection between chemistry and physics. *Kinetic* is a word that means movement. The theory explains why substances behave as they do by looking at the physics of how molecules move. Kinetic theory explains that gases behave as they do because their molecules are moving about constantly. The theory also led to the science called **thermodynamics,** which means "heat in motion." Kinetic theory also explains how gases always expand to fill as much space, or volume, as they can. The moving gas molecules stop spreading out only when they hit a barrier, such as the side of a container. If the molecules of all substances were completely free to move about, they would all be gases.

Forces

A force is a pushing or pulling action. Magnetism is an example of a force. A magnet can pull pieces of metal toward it, as with the iron filings in this photo. A magnet can also attract or repel (push away) other magnets. The forces inside chemicals work in a similar way to magnetism but they act on the scale of atoms and molecules.

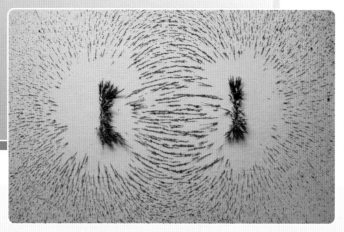

Gases expand to fill any available space, but solids and liquids do not. There must be some (**force**) that holds the molecules together more closely in liquids and solids than in gases. Many substances, such as salts and metals, are solids in which the molecules are held together very tightly. They have a regular crystal structure that prevents the molecules from moving around as much as they do in gases and liquids. In less structured solids and in liquids, the molecules are arranged more loosely and held together by weaker bonds. The weak forces that hold together (**liquids**) and noncrystalline solids are named van der Waals forces for their discoverer, (**Johannes Diderik van der Waals**).

Johannes Diderik van der Waals

When former Dutch schoolteacher Johannes Diderik van der Waals (1837–1923; right) published his first scientific results, the distinguished British physicist James Clerk Maxwell was impressed. Maxwell commented: "There can be no doubt that the name of Van der Waals will soon be among the foremost in molecular science." Maxwell was right. Van der Waals became the outstanding physicist of his day and won the prestigious Nobel Prize for physics in 1910.

Van der Waals helped to show that solids, liquids, and gases are all versions of fundamentally the same thing. For example, steam, water, and ice are all forms of water, but they behave in different ways due to the forces between the molecules. Van der Waals helped extend the kinetic theory by showing how the pressure, volume, and temperature of ordinary gases were linked by simple math.

Solids, Liquids, and Gases

The molecules in a solid are fixed loosely in place. They vibrate but do not move around widely. Molecular forces such as van der Waals forces keep the molecules in position. When a solid such as ice is heated, the molecules gain energy and vibrate more energetically. Eventually the heat gives the molecules enough energy to overcome the molecular forces. When the forces can no longer hold the molecules in place, they start to move more freely. The solid ice melts into liquid water. If the liquid is heated further, the molecules move about more freely still and the liquid vaporizes into a gas.

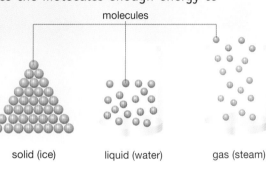

molecules

solid (ice)   liquid (water)   gas (steam)

Valency

Chemical bonds hold molecules in compounds together. The valency of an atom explains how many bonds, or links, it can form with other atoms to make compounds. Water has the chemical symbol H_2O, which shows that two hydrogen atoms link up with a single oxygen atom (below). In each molecule of water, two hydrogen atoms link to a single oxygen atom. The valency of hydrogen is one, so each hydrogen atom can link to only one other atom. Oxygen has a valency of two, so each oxygen atom can link to two other atoms. Different elements have a different valency. Carbon has a valency of four, which means it can make links with up to four other atoms.

oxygen atom (has a valency of 2)

hydrogen atoms (each has a valency of 1)

Van der Waals forces are weak links between molecules. The chemical bonds that lock atoms together in molecules involve much stronger forces. American chemist Gilbert Lewis (1875–1946) was one of the scientists who did most to explain chemical bonds. He played a key role in developing an important theory called (valency.) This theory explains why elements join in different proportions to form compounds. Valency advances and explains the ideas put forward earlier by both Dalton and Gay-Lussac.

The theory of valency had another important impact. A German chemist named Friedrich Kekulé (1829–1896) found that carbon always has a valency of four. This discovery led him to make a number of important discoveries about the chemistry of carbon and also formulate a famous theory about benzene. Most important of all, Kekulé found that carbon could link into very long and complicated chains.

Carbon chemistry is important because carbon is the basis for all living things. By 1900, Kekulé's work had spawned the new field of organic chemistry. This paved the way for two of the most important scientific discoveries of the twentieth century: photosynthesis, or how plants make food from sunlight, and the structure of DNA, the genetic (inherited) material in the cells of living things.

Benzene Ring

Benzene is used in the manufacture of many products, from explosives to nylon and plastics to antiseptics. Kekulé was the first person to realize that the structure of a molecule of benzene is based on a ring of six carbon atoms (below; gray). He said the idea came to him when he dreamed about a snake, coiled into a circle, biting its own tail.

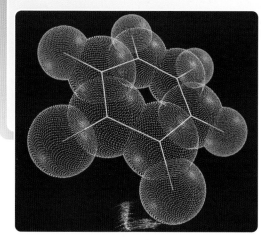

Organic Chemistry

Organic chemistry is the study of carbon and its compounds. In the twentieth century, organic chemistry proved to be one of the most important and far-reaching branches of chemistry. Organic chemistry is crucial to such important industrial applications as oil refining. It is also used in the manufacture of plastics (below). Plastics are formed by long chains of carbon-based molecules called polymers.

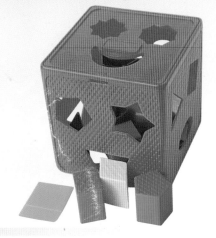

5 INSIDE THE ATOM

Molecules form when atoms combine. But what forms atoms? Toward the end of the nineteenth century, the discovery of radioactivity led to scientists' first real glimpse inside the atom.

WHILE SOME SCIENTISTS SOUGHT to better understand the mysteries of molecules, others were probing deeper into the atom. The word *atom* once meant something that could not be split.

A series of important discoveries by scientists in the late nineteenth century suggested the idea of the indivisible atom was too simple. New discoveries gave scientists new insights.

Radioactivity

Most elements have stable atoms that are held together effectively by strong bonds. Some elements are less stable. Unstable elements, such as uranium, give off radioactivity. Radioactivity is tiny energetic particles that fire out from an atom at great speed. The particles can be detected by a Geiger counter (below). When the atom has given off all its radioactive particles, it becomes stable, or nonradioactive.

Marie Curie

Marie Curie (below) was born in Poland in 1867. She moved to Paris and started to work with radioactivity around her thirtieth birthday. No one then knew about the dangers of radioactivity. Curie died in 1934 from leukemia, a cancer of the blood. Her illness was most likely caused by years of exposure to radiation through her work. Radiation has since been used by doctors to kill cancerous cells and has helped extend the lives of millions of people.

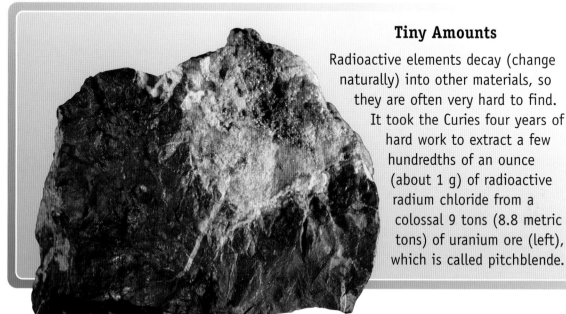

Tiny Amounts

Radioactive elements decay (change naturally) into other materials, so they are often very hard to find. It took the Curies four years of hard work to extract a few hundredths of an ounce (about 1 g) of radioactive radium chloride from a colossal 9 tons (8.8 metric tons) of uranium ore (left), which is called pitchblende.

Radioactivity was discovered accidentally in 1896. French physicist Antoine Henri Becquerel (1852–1908) chanced upon radioactivity when he left a lump of uranium ore, called pitchblende, on top of a photographic plate. Radioactivity from the uranium caused a ghostly image of the pitchblende to appear on the photographic plate.

The following year, a young French physicist named **Marie Curie** began to explore radiation. Curie and her husband, Pierre, processed huge amounts of ore to extract **tiny amounts** of radioactive materials for her to study. Curie discovered two new radioactive elements: polonium (which was named for Poland, the country where she was born) and radium.

Rutherford's Recognition

New Zealand-born physicist Ernest Rutherford (1871–1937; right) performed most of his famous experiments on atoms and radioactivity while he worked at Cambridge University in England. The importance of his work was recognized in many ways. Rutherford won the Nobel Prize for physics in 1908, and the king knighted him Sir Ernest Rutherford in 1914. When Rutherford died in 1937, he was buried in Westminster Abbey, London, alongside Sir Isaac Newton, Charles Darwin, and the kings and queens of England.

Thanks to the work of **Ernest Rutherford** and his colleagues, the study of radioactivity soon began to provide insights into the structure of the atom. If radioactive atoms gave off particles, then atoms must be built from smaller particles. When unstable atoms change into stable ones, some of these particles are thrown out. It was these particles that scientists such as Marie Curie had detected being given off by radioactive substances. By 1900, Rutherford had discovered that there were three different types of **radiation.** In 1911 Rutherford carried out a famous experiment when he fired radiation at a very thin piece of **gold foil.** The results of this experiment led Rutherford to suggest the theory of the nuclear atom, or the idea that every atom has a dense positively charged nucleus at its center, surrounded by space.

Types of Radiation

Rutherford discovered three types of radiation given off by atoms: alpha particles, beta particles, and gamma rays. An alpha particle has the same structure as the nucleus of a helium atom. It consists of two protons (particles with a positive electrical charge) and two neutrons (particles with no charge). A beta particle is the same thing as an electron (a particle with a negative charge). It is smaller and travels faster and farther than an alpha particle. Gamma rays are similar to X rays, radio waves, and other kinds of electromagnetic radiation. Gamma rays travel long distances and pass right through solid objects.

Rutherford's Gold Foil Experiment

Rutherford and his assistant Ernest Marsden fired alpha particles at thin gold foil. Most of the alpha particles passed right through, as Rutherford had expected, but some bounced straight back. Rutherford said: "It was as though you had fired a fifteen-inch shell at a piece of tissue paper and it had bounced back and hit you." Alpha particles have a positive charge. They would bounce back only if the atoms in the gold foil also contained a large concentrated positive charge.

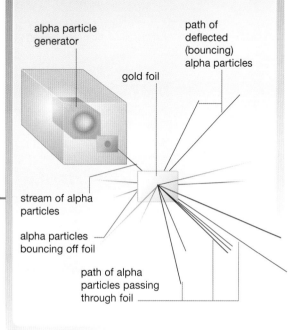

alpha particle generator

path of deflected (bouncing) alpha particles

gold foil

stream of alpha particles

alpha particles bouncing off foil

path of alpha particles passing through foil

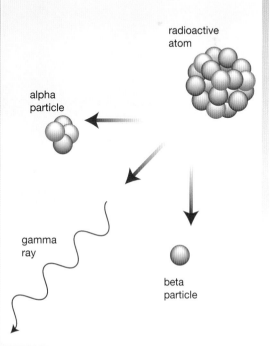

radioactive atom

alpha particle

gamma ray

beta particle

Rutherford the Alchemist?

Ernest Rutherford proved it was possible to change one element into another by splitting the atom. He fired alpha particles at nitrogen atoms. The particles split some of the nitrogen atoms into smaller hydrogen and oxygen atoms. Rutherford's aims and methods differed from those of the alchemists, but by changing one element into another, he achieved their goal of transmutation. The vital difference was his approach: Alchemists tried to change elements using chemical reactions; Rutherford split nitrogen atoms physically by firing particles at them.

J.J. Thomson

J.J. Thomson is remembered most for his discovery of the electron in 1897. It was his most startling discovery. Thomson taught at Cambridge University, England, where he worked with Ernest Rutherford. Thomson had once championed the plum pudding theory of atomic structure (below). It was while working with Thomson that Rutherford disproved the plum pudding theory by performing his gold foil experiment.

electron   atom

A few years before (Rutherford's) famous gold foil experiment, British physicist (J.J. Thomson) (1856–1940), discovered a new particle. It became known as the (electron.) Electrons are far smaller than atoms and carry tiny amounts of negative charge. Thomson wondered where electrons fit into the atom. He believed that atoms were made up like plum puddings. The electrons were "plums" dotted randomly inside a much larger mass of positive matter, the "pudding."

Rutherford's gold foil experiment proved that Thomson's picture of the atom was wrong. The positive matter in an atom had to be concentrated in its center, not scattered throughout the atom. With Rutherford's help, Danish physicist Niels Bohr (1885–1962) put together a new picture of the atom in 1913. Far from being uncuttable, as the original meaning of the word atom suggested, atoms seemed to be built from three kinds of smaller particles. Atoms were not, after all, the basic building blocks of matter. Inside an atom were (subatomic particles) called electrons, protons, and neutrons. In Bohr's model of the atom, a central nucleus held the protons and neutrons while electrons whizzed around the outer space of the atom.

The Bohr Model of Subatomic Particles

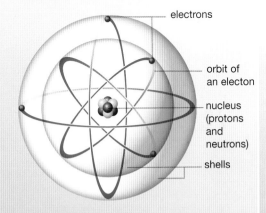

- electrons
- orbit of an electon
- nucleus (protons and neutrons)
- shells

Electrons

If atoms are small, then electrons are almost unimaginably tiny. Even the smallest atoms are more than a thousand times the size of an electron. If it were possible to scale up an electron so it weighed as much as an apple, and an apple could be scaled up by the same amount, the resulting apple would weigh about one million times as much as Earth.

Atoms are composed of three types of subatomic particles: protons, neutrons, and electrons. There are approximately the same number of protons and neutrons in an atom, and there are exactly the same number of protons as electrons. Protons and neutrons form the central core of an atom, called the nucleus. Protons are positively charged, neutrons have no charge, and electrons are negatively charged. Protons and neutrons clump together tightly in the nucleus. Much of the rest of an atom is empty space. According to the Bohr model (above), electrons move around the nucleus a little like planets orbit the Sun. During their orbit, electrons occupy defined areas called shells.

6 INTO THE FUTURE

Scientists may never form a complete understanding of atoms and molecules, but they have learned enough to develop many practical technologies from the theories of atomic physics.

ALMOST A CENTURY AFTER Rutherford's famous experiments, the picture of the atom is still not complete. In 1913 Bohr put forward the idea that electrons moved in orbits around the nucleus. This theory proved to be too simple. In the 1920s, a set of new ideas called (**quantum theory**) suggested that

Quantum Theory

Quantum theory is an attempt to explain the mysterious world inside the atom. The theory is based on the idea that energy exists in fixed-sized packets called quanta. A single packet of energy is called a quantum. One of the ideas behind quantum theory is that electrons behave sometimes as particles and at other times like a wave.

Particle Accelerators

A particle accelerator is a bit like an immensely long cannon. Instead of shooting shells, it uses huge amounts of energy to fire subatomic particles at each other. When the particles collide, they explode in a shower of smaller particles.

Murray Gell-Mann

Murray Gell-Mann (1929–) won the 1969 Nobel Prize for physics (below, on right) for his quark theory. Gell-Mann believes a great scientist must have two qualities. He calls these qualities "good taste" and "killer instinct." Good taste means picking the right problems to work on. The killer instinct involves pursuing ideas with utter determination.

Quarks

Scientists theorize that quarks are the basic particles from which protons and neutrons are made. There are six types of quarks and they have rather unusual names: top, bottom, up, down, charm, and strange. No one has yet seen a quark, but experiments and theories suggest they must exist.

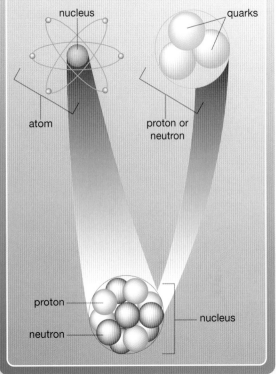

electrons did not always behave like particles. Sometimes they act as waves and spread out like a fuzzy cloud.

As scientists gained a greater understanding of the atom, they realized that its structure was more complex than they had thought previously. (**Particle accelerators**) helped physicists discover new particles inside the atom. In the 1960s, the American physicists (**Murray Gell-Mann**) and

George Zweig proposed that protons and neutrons are each composed of more fundamental particles, which they called (**quarks**.) Protons and neutrons are made up of quarks, but whether quarks really are the basic building blocks of matter remains to be proven.

The twentieth century was often called the atomic age. Scientists still had questions about the structure of atoms, but they knew enough to put them to productive use. Studies by scientists such as Ernest Rutherford and Marie Curie led to the idea that atoms would give off massive amounts of energy when they broke apart. The most spectacular demonstration of this was the invention of the **atomic bomb** during World War II (1939–1945). People later harnessed the power of atoms for peaceful purposes. The first **atomic power plants** to produce electricity were built in the 1950s.

Atomic Bomb

Some radioactive atoms decay by splitting into smaller, more stable atoms, and release a burst of energy as they do so. Under certain conditions, a single reaction sets off others in a chain of other reactions. The chain reaction generates a colossal amount of energy that provides the huge explosive power of an atomic bomb. Just 2.2 pounds (1 kg) of uranium can make an explosion like that produced by 17,000 tons (17,270 metric tons) of conventional explosive.

Chernobyl Controversy

At first, people heralded nuclear power as the fuel of the future. Dirty coal-fired power stations could be replaced with seemingly clean nuclear reactors. The image of nuclear power was tarnished, however, by accidents and leaks, such as one in 1979 at Three Mile Island, Pennsylvania (above). Even greater realization of the risks of radioactivity came in 1986 when the world's worst nuclear accident hit the Chernobyl power plant in Ukraine. A cloud of radioactive gas covered much of Europe. Livestock was affected as far away as northern Europe. An unknown number of people in Ukraine and surrounding areas died of radiation-induced illnesses such as cancer.

The twenty-first century may prove to be the age of the molecule. Scientists once had to rely on searching for useful substances in nature, usually by accident. Now they use computers to design whole new molecules. Drugs are designed from scratch to have the right properties to cure particular diseases. Strong and lightweight materials engineered for cutting-edge applications such as space technology and deep-sea exploration can also be exploited for regular use.

Chemists are today at the forefront of technology that uses molecules in entirely new and exciting ways. One such important new field is the science of **nanotechnology**. The study of atoms and molecules has come a long way, but it is far from over.

Nanotechnology

Nanotechnology involves building microscopic structures from atoms and molecules. One intriguing use might be to make miniature machines that travel inside the human body to carry out ultraprecise operations. Nanomachines like this could be built from tiny pieces called nanotubes (below). Nanotubes are sheets of carbon rolled into cylinders just a few nanometers across. One nanometer is about one-thousandth the width of a human hair. The cylinders can be joined together to make a nanomachine.

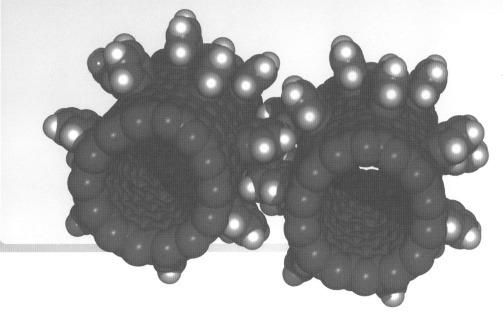

Glossary

alchemy An early form of chemistry which aimed to turn ordinary metals into gold.

alpha particle Large radioactive particle identical to the nucleus of a helium atom.

apeiron Universal substance thought to form all matter by Anaximander.

atom The smallest particle of a chemical element.

base metal Metal such as lead that alchemists tried to turn into gold.

bond The force that holds atoms together in a molecule.

caloric theory An early theory that suggested heat was a substance that flowed like a liquid.

compound A chemical substance made by joining different elements.

chemistry The science of studying the composition, structure, and properties of substances, and the changes they undergo.

electrolysis A method of separating a compound into its elements using electricity.

electron A tiny, negatively charged particle that exists inside atoms.

element A chemical that cannot be separated into simpler substances using only chemical means.

force A pushing or pulling action.

kinetic theory The idea that substances behave as they do because of the moving molecules within them.

mass The amount of matter.

matter The substance from which things are made.

molecule A structure made by joining two or more atoms.

nanotechnology A method of building microscopic machines from atoms or molecules.

neutron An uncharged particle in the nucleus of an atom.

nucleus The central part of an atom.

organic chemistry The study and practical uses of carbon and its compounds.

particle accelerator Machine that makes particles move very fast before smashing them together to reveal their subatomic contents.

periodic table A way of arranging the chemical elements so that ones with similar properties are grouped in columns.

physics The science of studying matter and energy and the ways they interact.

proton A positively charged particle in the nucleus of an atom.

quantum A packet of energy. Two or more quantums are called quanta.

quantum theory The theory of the microscopic world inside atoms.

quark A basic particle from which larger particles such as protons and neutrons are made.

radioactivity The particles given off when unstable atoms decay (or change) into smaller, more stable atoms.

reaction A chemical change in which one set of elements and compounds (the reactants) turns into a different set of elements and compounds (the products).

relative atomic mass The mass of an atom compared to the mass of one-twelfth of a carbon atom. This gives hydrogen a value of 1 unit.

shell The orbit occupied by an electron as it circuits a nucleus.

subatomic particle Particles that together form an atom, such as electrons, protons, and neutrons.

thermodynamics study of the transfer of energy, in the form of heat, during chemical reactions.

transmutation In alchemy, turning one material into another.

valency The number of chemical bonds that an atom can form with other atoms.

For More Information

BOOKS

Nick Arnold. *Chemical Chaos*. New York: Scholastic, 1998.

Peter Atkins. *The Periodic Kingdom: A Journey into the Land of Chemical Elements*. New York: Basic Books, 1997.

Christopher Cooper. *Eyewitness: Matter*. New York: Dorling Kindersley, 2000.

Jill Frankel Hauser. *Super Science Concoctions: 50 Mysterious Mixtures for Fabulous Fun*. New York: Williamson, 2003.

Robert C. Mebane and Thomas R. Rybolt. *Adventures with Atoms and Molecules: Chemistry Experiments for Young People*. Berkeley Heights, NJ: Enslow, 1998.

Albert Stwertka. *A Guide to the Elements*. New York: Oxford Children's Books, 2002.

Janice VanCleave. *Janet VanCleave's Chemistry for Every Kid: 101 Easy Experiments that Really Work*. Indianapolis, IN: John Wiley & Sons, 1999.

WEBSITES

Cambridge Physics
www.cambridgephysics.com/
Information about the splitting of the atom and the discovery of the electron.

CERN Education
visitsservice.web.cern.ch/VisitsService/education/oresources.html
Lots of information about subatomic particles.

Java Applets for Chemistry
www.edinformatics.com/il/il_chem.htm
Virtual chemistry experiments you can run on your computer.

Rader's Chem4kids
www.chem4kids.com/
Tutorials on atoms, matter, elements, and chemical reactions.

Web Elements
www.webelements.com/
An online periodic table, with key information for every element.

Index